Jesus Without Christianity

Book I

Jesus Without Christianity

Book 1

The Original Pre-Christian Master and His Lost Teachings

Christopher Lepine

Soulscape Publishing

Jesus Without Christianity

The Original Pre-Christian Master and His Lost Teachings

By
Christopher Lepine

Published by:
Soulscape Publishing
1566 Greenbriar Blvd.
Boulder, CO 80305

First paperback edition 2026
ISBN: 978-1-964822-00-6

To my dear Divine Master, my father-brother, our Son of God who revealed our loving Universal Father and brought His eternal, liberating truth, as Jesus of Nazareth.

I owe you my life and give you all that I am for the adventure of eternity.

Contents

Come to me, all you who are weary and burdened, and I will give you rest. Take my yoke upon you and learn from me, for I am gentle and humble in the heart, and you will find rest for your souls. For my yoke is easy and my burden is light.

–Jesus, from *The Bible*
(Matthew 11:28)

Introduction

Reclaiming Your Divine Treasure

You have a hunger and curiosity about Jesus, and you're not alone: modern global interest was never higher. The key is to know and follow Jesus first without Christianity. You must go with Jesus above and beyond Christianity and apply these lessons to life and any spiritual community you value, especially Christian churches.

This book shows you how to know the Divine Master and follow his guidance. You can find peace, joy, confidence, power, adventure, and satisfaction to the depths of your eternal soul.

Jesus is not the property of any religion, race, political party, or nation, but the true Master for humanity.

His presence, love, and transforming power **can be yours directly** without any intervening person or group. No one has the right to interfere with or interpret your experience with the Divine Master and God!

If you're here for academic study, you won't be satisfied. But, if you want direct personal contact with the divine-human Master known as "Jesus," you'll find the tools to satisfy your hunger and have amazing life-changing spiritual experiences.

I wrote this book for all sincere truthseekers who want to grow. Whether you're a non-Christian or Christian, whatever your background–culture, race, profession, or experience, you'll find a liberating and enlightening revelation of Jesus. God's door of life is open to all: His main concern is your intentions and willingness to be like him.

Jesus is not a Christian, nor can we assume that he agrees with those teachings and practices, or the opinions and activities of any Christian church or Christian. Jesus was a divine being before Christianity, gave his perfect teachings, and is the divine gateway to the Creator of the universe–God, our loving Divine Father.

It's time to liberate ourselves for new lives based on the real Jesus and His original hidden pre-Christian teachings that he meant for the world: Much of what you've been taught about Jesus and God the Father is wrong.

This book will show you how to find and benefit from the greatest knowledge in the world: the original life and teachings of Jesus.

I use two sources: Quotations from Jesus from the most important Christian book, *The Bible*, and quotations from Jesus and information about him from *The Urantia Book*–a profound revelation written by angels in the Twentieth Century.

If you keep an *open mind and listen* to The Spirit of Truth within you, you'll discover what's true and open the door to your true destiny. This can begin a new chapter in your life of peace, joy, liberation, empowerment, and success. This can be the gateway to profound spiritual experiences and wonderful changes.

This book shares the remarkable prefect recipe from Jesus and the electrifying inspiration of his God-centered life. *You'll find soul-satisfying truth that can change your life.* This book is a journey of discovery to every part of the life and teachings of Jesus–without Christianity, before Christianity.

Chapter 1–The Limitations of Christianity, reveals the errors after Jesus and their negative impacts. *Chapter 2–The Direct Steps to Jesus*, gives the keys to get to the real truth about the Master. *Chapter 3–Who is Jesus?*, explores where he came from, who he really is, and the mission of his earth life. *Chapter 4–The Original Teachings of Jesus*, shares the lost, liberating, fair pathway to God for a meaningful and great life. In *Chapter 5–*

Living with Jesus without Christianity, you'll learn and be inspired by Jesus and understand the amazing future you can choose.

Open your heart and mind with a sincere desire for truth and growth, and prepare for delight. Your life is a gift from God, and no one has the right to judge your spiritual worth or tell you what to think or do. No one has the right to interfere with your relationship with God. So, take whatever value you can find from this book and move forward.

You have tremendous inner, divine gifts. You are known, loved, and valued by God. You can find a life more rewarding than you can imagine. The keys are simple. The way is open.

Let's begin the fascinating journey and remove the haze of 20 centuries to see the light of the real Jesus and his original teachings.

Of all human knowledge, that which is of greatest value is to know the religious life of Jesus and how he lived it.

–*The Urantia Book*
(196:1:3)

The Limitations of Christianity

The Errors and Middlemen

Chapter 1

You are a child of God, and He wants you to know Him directly. He wants you to take the adventure of finding the truth and making decisions for yourself. This is the sacred gift of self-consciousness and personal decision-dignity, the interplay between yourself, God, and the outer life of body and world.

This is your eternal birthright from the Creator–The Universal Father, and *no one has the right to interfere*. No one has the right to judge your spiritual worth or tell you what to think or do.

Don't let anyone rob you of this eternal gift.

This is the very center of the life and teachings of Jesus, the God-Man independent of all religions and human institutions. He is a pure divine light from above.

God is your source and destiny and should get your highest loyalty. He loves you as if you were the only being in the universe. He has an amazing destiny for you and creates the fire for truth and growth that burns within your soul. His spirit lives within your mind and is your teacher and direct link to him.

God will give you everything you need, when you need it, where you need it, the way you need it, for as long as you need it. And, finding the divine Jesus directly is a very strong need and a key to finding God the Father.

You have a right to know the truth about Jesus. It's time for you to find his pre-Christian brilliant teachings: They are destined to transform all of us and the world. Jesus is more amazing than you can imagine and is now your divine friend who successfully lived his mission on earth: He is the Way, the Truth, and the Life.

The Hunger for God

You are a child of God, and we are family. You have a unique, eternal destiny, and God draws you to it with a steady desire for truth and growth. This hunger for God is the hope for a better life and is *only satisfied with a direct experience of Him, and a life of trying to follow His guidance:* The Father placed his spirit in your mind to show you the way and to transform you.

The Divine Father–the Creator–yearns for a relationship with you, and the Divine Jesus is the bridge to Him. Jesus also longs for a relationship with you and gives his Spirit of Truth to help you find, live, and speak the truth. His perfect teachings are the ultimate guide and lead to a happy life now and an endless adventure after death.

Studying the life of Jesus is the ultimate way to understand the person of God the Father.

When you look at how Jesus lived on earth, you are looking at how God the Father would live and relate to others in human form.

To get to the original teachings and person of Jesus, we need to listen to the ring of truth from the Spirit of Truth within. Whether you're reading, seeing, or listening to someone or something, the Spirit of Truth that Jesus gave you will let you know if it's true.

We need to turn off the noise in our lives and make room to talk to and listen to God. We need to remove any layers or filters that interfere with listening to potential new truth, and most of all, hearing the Spirit of Truth.

Don't let anything limit your birthright. Whether you had a bad experience with a parent, a church or organization, whether you're disgusted by so-called followers of Jesus who do not live his teachings, no matter what's happened to you, bravely find the truth and the life God meant for you. Free your mind of the debris and smoke so you can see the light of truth.

Christianity is not exactly what Jesus taught: It's filled with many errors, prejudices, and practices that Jesus never advocated. Much of what you've been told about Jesus and God the Father is wrong. And the mistakes, abuses, and distortions of the Christian Church through the centuries caused not only a revolt against the Church, but against God Himself. Modern popular prejudices and indifference to God polluted our thinking and is a barrier to finding the real Jesus and true happiness.

If the early followers of Jesus had taught **exactly** what he taught and did not later attach a flawed, controlling church or judge the morals or religious practices of others, the original teachings of Jesus would have been adopted be every race, culture, and nation: We would have a dramatically-better world.

The greatest knowledge is to know the original life and teachings of Jesus. This will transform the world.

We need to liberate ourselves. We need to find Jesus without Christianity.

The Modern Spiritual Crisis

The moral and spiritual foundations of Western civilization are *quickly* crumbling. Less and less is valued and passed down from generation to generation. These teachings and practices from Judaism, and especially Christianity, are being devalued and aren't as effective as they once were.

The ruthless waves of relentless modern changes and challenges are eroding the sandcastle. Huge numbers of people around the world are spiritually malnourished or in starvation and losing their desire for the spiritual food they so badly need. The old teachings and institutions are flawed, but the big problem is that we don't have better life instructions that will unify and stimulate us to build a better world.

The results are nothing short of tragic, and if not fixed, mean the continued loss of the good in human relationships and our collective civilization. Catastrophe and suffering are becoming more frequent. Read any news source and you're bombarded with increasingly bad news about people, groups, nations, and the planet.

Our spiritual knowledge and practices are tattered and weak in the face of the modern world. Countless millions are lost, trapped in a labyrinth of insecurity, fear, depression, lack of motivation and direction, sadness, and pain. The hunger is profound and growing. The Christian explanation that has worked for over 2,000 years in the West and elsewhere is no longer persuasive, and is rejected by most.

The younger a person, the more likely they are to avoid any formal religion and its teachings.

And, it is likely that even those who are starving and find initial illumination and joy in Christianity, will, as they mature in their spiritual life, eventually find dissatisfaction years later. They will yearn for the real Jesus and his original teachings.

The majority of people across the globe are troubled and dissatisfied. As a human species we are in the greatest crisis of our existence. The more someone lives in the world of modern thought and technology, the more likely they are to be dissatisfied and in pain, hungering for a better explanation of the purpose of their life and the way to live.

People need a new spiritual explanation for the big questions: Who am I? Where did I come from? Where am I going? Who is God? What is the purpose of my life? How do I find true happiness? Why is the world the way it is? How do I leave a true legacy? How can I make a difference and help others?

When you discover the real person and original teachings of Jesus, *you'll find the answers.* Since Christianity has been the main source of knowledge about Jesus and his teachings, we need to carefully *locate and remove* the distortions and errors. We must find the seed of the original teachings of Jesus and discover this real God-Man.

The Mistakes of Christianity

Finding Jesus and his original teachings directly is the gateway to a better life and requires us to understand where Christianity went wrong.

Keep your mind open.

For those with a Christian background, the key now is **putting God first** above any church, group, or person, and **trusting** His spirit within to show the truth. For those without a Christian background, the key is to **be patient** and gradually extract Jesus from the Christian presentation in your thinking.

This book doesn't judge Christians, but it's time for a clear assessment of what happened after Jesus finished his earth life.

Once we remove the distortions and errors it will be easier to find the real teachings and person of Jesus. The apostles and the later Christians gave a religion that transformed the entire Western world, but humankind was robbed of the original, divine teachings of the Master.

Many sacrificed their fortunes and lives for God–to Jesus, and the world is indebted. The courage of these women and men is astounding, and Jesus appreciates their devotion. But our ultimate loyalty must be to God and the truth, not to any human, tradition, religion, group, nation, or race.

The early Christians did the best they could, but they made mistakes and calculated compromises, and many abused their power. The gigantic, totalitarian Roman Catholic church and many of its denominational offspring eventually became enmeshed with power, politics, and the everyday secular world.

Today, the majority of Christian churches weakly relate to what Jesus originally taught. Sadly, some of them oppose his teachings, but claim to follow him, preferring their unhealthy personal values and agendas. The vast array of Christian churches is well-meaning, but becoming more and more distant from Jesus, more like the dominant materialistic culture: They are dying off.

So, how did the followers of Jesus get off track?

The first big mistake was from the Apostles when they taught that the focus should be on the worship of Jesus and the miracle of his resurrection. They created a *religion about Jesus*, instead of sharing the *religion of Jesus* that he painstakingly taught them. Later Christians only amplified this distortion, drowning out the music the Master first gave us.

The Christian leader, Paul of Tarsus, championed the primitive idea that all humans are tainted with sin at birth and could only be saved through a blood sacrifice, namely, the death of Jesus. He taught that man was separated from God the Father and that only way each of us could connect with God and remove the barrier of inherited sin was to be cleansed in the blood of Christ (Jesus); we could then have full relationship with God.

Paul was a truly great and brave man who gave and suffered much and is the organizational genius and driving force of early Christianity. He helped many millions find spiritual comfort, but his writings clearly state a distorted, barbaric, repugnant view of God the Father that have confused and alienated countless millions for hundreds of years.

This theology has no place in the real teachings of Jesus, the presentation of a loving fair God, our kind and just Father.

And, in the name of growth, Christianity made many compromises in ancient times with pagan cults such as Mithraism, and incorporated some of those beliefs and ritual elements. The quest for power and the total control of every person in the Christian sphere gave birth to some of the worst atrocities and abuses in human history.

It's no surprise that today's family of Christianity is a faint and troubled shadow of what Jesus lived and taught. The reality of the modern world is fully revealing these troubles and cries out for the real Jesus. Many voices within Christianity agree and are trying to find a new way.

But, have no doubt, *Jesus loves each and every Christian and is trying to help all of them* to understand the true nature of God and to discover his original teachings directly.

The Direct Jesus Experience

Our thoughts are the doorways to find the truth about Jesus. His Spirit of Truth within you will tell you what is true if you trust with the sincerity and intensity of a little child. God will help you peel away the layers of misconceptions, prejudices, and distortions in your thinking holding you back from the life you were meant to live.

Jesus taught that the Creator of the universe is your loving, perfect, Heavenly Father who wants to have a relationship with you. We are His children–family. His spirit lives within you and gives you direct contact and guidance with Him. All that you need is **faith–acceptance** of God's message to you that you are His child. Your sincere hunger for truth and a desire for growth opens the door for God to send His message and assurance.

All you need to do is believe. All you need to do is accept the truth. Use your faith–the spiritual certainty that God gives you.

The purpose of our lives should be to find and follow the guidance of God, the will of The Universal Father. **There can be no greater privilege, joy, or satisfaction.** The rewards–the fruits of the spirit–are unlimited and continue from here to eternity.

Those are the original teachings of Jesus. The focus is God the Father. The way to find God is through sincere faith-acceptance of the truth that you are His child. Eternal life is made possible by following God's will so you can grow and give.

The religion of Jesus means a life filled with joy and is focused on *service* to others. It will ultimately transform each person, enable us to solve our problems, and bring a world beyond our dreams.

I am the bread of life: He that cometh to me shall never hunger; and he that believeth on me shall never thirst.

–Jesus, from *The Bible*
(John 6:35)

The Direct Steps to Jesus

Escaping the Monopoly

Chapter 2

You want to know Jesus, and he wants you to come home to him. His way is simple and **does not require translators or middlemen** . . . or a church. And, he won't tolerate anyone who tries to interfere with his personal relationship with you.

Over the centuries since Jesus' resurrection, the Christian churches convinced most people that they had a reliable version of his teachings and that *the only way to Jesus was through them*: You had to believe their interpretations, follow their rules, and support all they said and did. The Christian churches used this psychological monopoly at first in a sincere effort to help people, but often later as a cruel lever to judge, control, or exploit their members and others.

Most people still believe that Jesus founded Christianity and that it is how he wants them to find him. They often see Jesus and Christianity as ONE: They think Jesus supports everything that Christianity teaches and does.

But these misconceptions are beginning to fade–even from within Christianity. Sincere, progressive, and honest people want to know Jesus directly and the real truth about him. Christian churches are shrinking *very rapidly* as people flee to search elsewhere for real truths from Jesus and supportive spiritual communities that try to live his original teachings.

The key is to start with a direct encounter with Jesus and build an ongoing relationship with him. The Divine Son awaits you, and his

Spirit of Truth will bring you together. If you are willing, he will transform your life. If we are willing, he will give us the power and guidance to transform the world.

Jesus' Desire for You

This perfected Son of God longs for a full relationship with you. He does not require you to be perfect or follow complicated or unfair rules to find him. His way is simple. He is a manifestation of the Father, filled with love and mercy.

He wants you to bring your whole heart–a full effort–to find him and the Father. And he wants you to keep trying since inner revelation and growth take time. Persistence and patience are key as you cultivate the spiritual garden of your soul.

He will bring you peace, assurance, security, joy, confidence, and power. He will lead you to the Universal Father who will give you the salvation of His spirit within you. And this path will never end as you fulfill your amazing destiny into the wonderous eternal ages.

Jesus will stop at nothing to awaken you and support your spiritual growth. He never gives up. His spirit will reveal the truth about his teachings and help you to live and share it with others. His Spirit of Truth will bring you a new life of confidence, happiness, and power.

His path to salvation–given to him from the Father–is simple.

Your Daily Spiritual Recipe

Each day we need to take the steps to soul nourishment and exercise that lead to continual spiritual reawakening and never-ending growth. Like anything that you want to achieve, you'll need to plan and then carry out that plan *consistently*.

Achieving goals is most often a gradual process of repeated steps: Nothing is achieved without wholehearted effort and dedication.

Your spiritual life is no different.

You must recognize and enjoy the gift of growth along the way to your spiritual goals. Jesus and the Father will be there and reward you at every step. Every effort you make to grow, every effort you make to listen to and follow God, actually *increases your capacity* for spiritual blessings and can accelerate your growth.

Finding Jesus directly requires greater effort at first, but once you fully accept his spirit and discover the Father's spirit within you, spiritual habits take root and begin to yield fruit. You build momentum. The time you take in your spiritual practice might seem time-consuming and difficult, but it soon refreshes and energizes you to such an extent that you actually save time and find more happiness in your outer life.

Plan a time each day for private, uninterrupted time with God. Take these steps to experience our Son of God directly, to make friends with the matchless God-Man–Jesus, and be led to our Father's spirit within you: 1) Relax and meditate. 2) Be wholehearted. 3) Express your faith and hunger for growth. 4) Pour your heart out. 5) Ask Jesus for help. 6) Listen and BELIEVE. 7) Pray that you do this the next day.

Let's look at these steps in depth.

1. **Relax and meditate.** A relaxed, clear mind is the foundation of contact with Jesus. Find a private, quite place. As you're sitting or kneeling, take deep breaths and exhale slowly. Ask God's spirit within you to help you clear your mind and open your heart. At first, you probably won't be very effective in this meditation, but you will begin to make good progress.

   Don't look for perfection here. In the very beginning, you may only be able to calm down a little. But, as you do this more often, you'll get better at it. Any effort you make here will help you.

2. **Be wholehearted.** Once you've calmed and cleared your mind, you can express your innermost longings and feelings. When you're still, you're much more

able to give everything to the moment. Remember to put your whole heart into it, even if from time to time you get distracted or tired. Put all your energies into expressing yourself to the very depths of your being, and then completely open up to our Son of God–Jesus.

3. **Express your faith and hunger for growth.** As you sit there with God, accept the experience you're having and will continue to have. When you experience the presence of Jesus and our Father, accept what you're experiencing.

   BELIEVE.

   This is often the most difficult part of beginning your spiritual path. Many of us have been trained to only believe what our societies, religions, groups, or others tell us is true. All too many people will try to rob you of your spiritual experience. When you're in prayer and these doubts, disbeliefs, and prejudices come into your mind, don't look at them and dwell on them: They are meaningless vapors that will evaporate in the clear atmosphere of divine truth.

Clear your mind and let the truth from the Spirit of Truth from Jesus shine to change your thoughts. Make the effort to keep focusing on the new spiritual thoughts, and they will reveal a clearer reality. Let go of prejudices and preconceived notions about Jesus and the spiritual life.

4. **Pour out your heart.** As intensely and deeply as you can, tell Jesus you want to find him. Tell him everything that is on your mind: thoughts, emotions, desires, goals, problems, fears, dreams, anything that is concerning or enticing you.

I can't emphasize this enough: Use total intensity and depth in sharing your thoughts and feelings with Jesus. This will allow you to move into true prayer and be open to the leading and inspiration of Jesus and our Universal Father–God.

Always listen longer than you speak. The whole point is to get divine guidance and power. So, like any good conversation, you need to let the other person talk. You can't hear anything–can't really listen–until you stop talking, until you stop expressing. And this goes for the entire prayer process.

5. **Ask Jesus for help.** Ask our Son of God for help for yourself and others, your family and friends. Share the situations that you and others are facing, and ask God to give you the spiritual transformation to meet a challenge, to increase hope, to bring peace and spiritual healing, to bring power.

6. **Listen and BELIEVE.** You will begin to hear some of what Jesus and our Father having been saying to your soul all your life. Sincerely come with a hunger for truth and growth and accept that you are a child of our loving Universal Father. Accept that Jesus, our Son of God, is your Divine Brother in God's family. Believe that we are all sisters and brothers. Embrace the light and love within.

7. **Pray that you do this the next day.** Ask Jesus to help you talk with him at the same time each day. This will help you keep going. Schedule a time and private place to talk to Jesus. Establish this wonderful spiritual habit and follow the steps for deeper and deeper contact with Jesus and our Heavenly Father. Realize the full joy of knowing who you really are and how much God loves you.

You will discover Jesus directly! He will take your hand and lead you to a life of joy, adventure, and growth. He is your best friend and will reveal and lead you to our Universal Father–God.

Your Need for Truth

You are a seeker of truth. You have a deep hunger for the truth and personal growth. God created this hunger and will give you the food of spiritual truth. When you accept the primary truth that God is your Father and that we are all His children, you begin the endless adventure of truth seeking.

When you take time with God, you will begin to get nourished with His direct inner revelations to you. Jesus gave us his Spirit of Truth: It feeds our souls with truth directly and helps us recognize potential truth from others in the outer world of everyday life. Jesus will reveal the amount of truth we are capable of recognizing when we are willing to accept it.

Our spiritual growth depends on it. Our souls yearn for truth. Our true selves delight in comprehending and living the truth: The greatest truths we can know are about our loving

Father and how we can live our lives to serve him and others.

Jesus and the life he lived is the greatest revelation and the most valuable of all human knowledge. The most important thing we can study is the life and teachings of our Son of God. The most important thing we can do is to follow his **original teachings** and build spiritual communities for this purpose.

The divine Son of God who became Jesus loves you beyond comprehension and knows all the challenges you face and mistakes you've made. He shows that the ultimate human life is one dedicated to following the will of God–The Universal Father–for personal growth and service to all.

The first step in understanding his teachings is to understand who he really is before, during, and after his life on earth.

Jesus of Nazareth was indeed a strong and forceful personality; he was an intellectual power and a spiritual stronghold. His personality not only appealed to the spiritually minded women among his followers, but also to the educated and intellectual Nicodemus and to the hardy Roman soldier, the captain stationed on guard at the cross, who, when he had finished watching the Master die, said, "Truly, this was a Son of God." And red-blooded, rugged Galilean fishermen called him Master . . .

His was a dignified manhood; he was good, but natural. Jesus did not pose as a mild, sweet, gentle, and kindly mystic. His teaching was thrillingly dynamic. He not only *meant well*, but he went about actually *doing good*.

—*The Urantia Book*
(141:3:5-6)

Who is Jesus?

The Astounding Truth

Chapter 3

Who was Jesus before he came to earth? Who was Jesus on earth? Who is Jesus now? What is the significance of Jesus for each person and humankind? The answers can transform you.

But you must have an open mind.

Suspend your disbelief, even if some ideas are uncomfortable or implausible to you, or might even make you anxious. Please be patient: The Spirit of Truth within you will give you the ring of truth at the right times. You'll *feel* it.

Trust God despite any of your negative experiences or previous beliefs.

Have faith and loyalty to God above any group, church, or person, and you'll be rewarded with the sweet nectar of truth. Take back what's yours.

I'm going to quote Jesus directly from the Christian *Bible* since this gives the most reliable human record of his teachings, although there are potential errors. All other *Bible* quotes are subject to more errors–interpretation, editing, and potential distortion–despite many who say it's the absolute "word of God." We'll see there's often a big difference between what Jesus and his followers taught.

Fear not. Your relationship to Jesus will only get deeper. Your admiration and devotion to him will only grow. Your life will only get better if you let his Spirit of Truth set you free.

But I need you to be even more open-minded and brave to consider the full truth about Jesus from another source: I'm going use quotations from and about Jesus from *The*

Urantia Book. You probably haven't heard of this book, but it's a new spiritual revelation destined to transform our thinking about and relation to Jesus.

We're going to remove 20 centuries of manmade debris to uncover the truth about Jesus. We'll start with the deepest, most important truth.

The Real Nature of God

The first step to free our minds to find the real Jesus is to think about his "Heavenly Father"–our Creator–in profoundly new ways. *Our view of Jesus and the way he lived and the reason for his cruel death is distorted by false teachings about God.* So, we need to learn what Jesus originally taught about God. This is the ultimate lens to reveal the life of Jesus and for the foundation of a glorious, joyful life.

Jesus taught and demonstrated that God is infinitely, incomprehensibly better than the best, most loving, fair, powerful, and capable being you can imagine. God–the Creator of the all–is a real being who can communicate with other people and has no flaws. God is perfect, all-powerful, fair, merciful, all-knowing, everywhere present, and above all, **LOVING**.

Above all aspects of God, the Creator is the most affectionate, loving being in the universe. God's overriding motivation is LOVE toward each of us on a personal, one-to-one, intimate level. This is the deepest and most important relationship we can have.

God does have laws, and there can be serious consequences to evil and selfish choices, but God's focus is love. He delights in nurturing and rewarding us for our good choices and never withholds his love, even when we make the wrong choices and rebel.

Anything else you've been taught about God is false. Listen to God's spirit within and find the truth and embrace God's presence. Your Creator yearns for your attention and will give you a never-ending revelation about Himself. Our gracious Father will supply all the guidance, power, and strength you need to do the joyous work of spiritual living–growth, service to others, and success.

Allow yourself to accept the truth within about your Divine Parent. Run and embrace God. Rip off the chains of false teachings and negative experiences or assumptions about God.

The Big Truths about God

When we accept the perfection and absolute love from God, we quickly rise above the smoke that obscures the light of truth and darkens our minds. **Remember, no one has the right to tell you what to think or do, or interfere with your relationship with God.** Trust the Creator's spirit within you to give the courage and flexibility to remove the errors of your thinking. Understand your birthright.

Let's look at eight key truths about God.

1. **God is a perfect, unlimited spiritual being.** God is perfect in every attribute of character. He is, and always will be, beyond what we can conceive of as the

perfect person. He is spirit and is unlimited, all-knowing, and all-powerful. God is the source of all. God existed before everything and decided to create everything.

2. **God is a real person.** God is not only the source and upholder of the universe and all people, but the planner of it all–a Father and friend. He is a real person who wants you to know Him *directly*. His Spirit is in you *right now* and waiting for you to accept and listen. God is self-conscious, has intentions, and exercises his will to unfold the infinite, eternal panorama of adventure. God is the ultimate personal being who is the everlasting source of all people. And his attitude towards us is pure love.

3. **God is loving and kind.** When we remember the perfection of God, then we know that the Creator doesn't get mad, frustrated, impatient, or vengeful. God is perfect; He has no flaws.

We've been told that God can punish us from His justified anger, but our loving Parent only acts with compassion, kindness, and fairness to give true justice and mercy. God is loving beyond comprehension and always forgives us, no matter what we do: God doesn't condone all we do, but the Creator is patient with us and knows all our challenges.

All actions from God are love-saturated and designed to help you grow and find true happiness in the amazing unique destiny He has for you. When you make mistakes or refuse to listen to God, He does all He can through *absolute love* to bring you back. There can be no limits to His love. He gives love without any conditions that you must meet. God is always remarkably kind, tender, and helpful.

4. **God is infinitely generous.** God always gives all the love and gifts you are

capable of perceiving and receiving. He will give you all you need, when you need it, in the way you need it, for as long as you need it. Limitations are imposed by our unwillingness to listen to and follow God. God's spirit lives within you and gives direct access to God. There is nothing that can separate you from God except your unspiritual decisions and thinking.

Our Divine Parent is the source and upholder of reality. God knows all from the eternal past, present, and future. He is before and is the source of time and space. God is The First Source and Center.

God has an infinite storehouse. No matter how vast the universe is and how many people are in it, the Creator will never run out of everything we need to build wonderful lives and have unending adventure . . . forever; God gives all and never runs out. God looks for every opportunity to give as much as we can benefit from. Our decisions can be the doorway to limitless blessings and *grow our capacity* to receive even more.

5. **God is fair and just.** God does not penalize or limit you based on the actions of others living or dead. *No human being is spiritually handicapped by the sin-decisions or actions of any being.* You were born with a completely fresh spiritual start with the gift of life, God's spirit within, the world around, and the ability to make decisions about all of it. Ultimately, people and things can slow you down, bring pain, joy, challenges, opportunities, and rewards, but nothing can keep you from God except your own decisions.

For I am persuaded, that neither death, nor life, nor angels, nor principalities, nor powers, nor things present, nor things to come, nor height, nor depth, nor any other creature, shall be able to separate us from the love of God, which is in Christ Jesus our Lord.

–The Apostle Paul, from *The Bible*, (Romans 8:38-39)

This is a beautiful, amazing quote from Paul, and I think, his best. It is true, so fundamental, that it is even more unfortunate that Paul got completely off track and introduced erroneous ideas about God, Jesus, and salvation.

The mistakes and sin-decisions of the human race do not produce some mystical black slime or collective karma that blocks God or suffocates your soul. God's love and generosity are infinite, but our reception of them is based on our willingness to listen to and follow Him. No baby is born with sin on her soul. God's universal spiritual presence surrounds us, and His spirit within guides us. What anyone has done or will do has no effect on this.

Paul's idea that we are born with sin on our souls that must be removed–atoned for–to have contact with God, is a barbaric, bizarre, and primitive concept. The concept of "Original Sin" is a grave error that grossly distorts many people's views of the infinitely fair and just Creator. The real God is always far beyond our highest, most ideal concepts of a loving Creator.

If we accept the idea that the innocent are punished for the sins of their ancestors, then the idea of justice and God takes a strange and revolting turn. This would mean that if you had a family, you'd be punishing your children for the mistakes made by their grandparents. Does it make sense for a kind and fair parent to withhold love from his children because of the long ago acts of their ancestors?

Unfortunately, this idea is promoted by Christianity and is an extremely intense core belief.

But, it gets even worse: That awful distortion of God was compounded by the teaching that the only way to overcome the separation of a person from God, no matter how kind or good the person, is for another being to absorb the mystical substance called sin . . . and be killed in human form in a remarkably cruel and painful and humiliating death.

The idea that God is this unfair and unjust and cruel has been and is a blasphemous betrayal to the love of God and a psychological barrier to hundreds of millions of struggling people.

Jesus never taught this distortion about his loving Heavenly Father.

Our loving, perfect, generous, patient, and kind Universal Father is not limited and never required that a divine son be sent to earth to become Jesus to become a blood sacrifice to make it possible for Him to contact us.

This is a cruel theological lie, a cancer on the spiritual life. It leads to confusion, fear, depression, and hopelessness. It tortures and shackles the lives of countless fear-ridden people in a dark, cold prison, blocking them from a fuller experience and a true understanding of God.

Our loving Father only requires that we spend time with him and try to follow His leading as best we can, to serve others and have personal achievement. **God's love is unconditional.** Jesus lived and taught the truths of these amazing divine gifts.

In the end, our decisions and actions determine whether we make progress and increase our happiness, or whether we go backwards in misery, or even in continuous rebellion to soul death.

These are the most important consequences in our lives, even though there are many negative and positive things we experience from the decisions of others. Ultimately, we determine how we will react to the inner experience of God and the outer experience of the world.

God is not directly punishing or rewarding us by determining events that impact our lives. We cannot control these, but we can grow closer to God, be more successful, and be more peaceful, confident, and powerful, and usually happier in the midst of all of them. *Our decisions determine our level of happiness and path through life.*

6. **God is beyond gender.** The Creator is an eternal, infinite being, the source of all things and beings in the universe.

God doesn't have gender and conform to the mold of what a human is. God is not male or female. He wasn't created in our image: We were created in His image.

God is definitely a real person who knows that He exists, makes decisions, takes action, and has relationships. He isn't bounded by human characteristics, but is the source of all of us and our gifts.

It's very hard to envision a being that isn't male or female. Everything we experience reflects this. For all of human existence, there have been male and female people. It's only natural that we think of God as having some gender. *Our entire language reflects this and is very limited.*

The important thing is for all of us to pick a name for God that reflects our own personal inner experience of the

Creator and not to judge others for the names they use for God. The concept of God is more important than the name.

7. **God is our loving Universal Father.** Jesus gave us and demonstrated the highest human concept of God: Father. The Master showed that God creates, provides for, strengthens, leads, protects, and loves *as a father*. Jesus taught this amazing truth through direct statements and parables, but most importantly, he demonstrated it with his life.

   God is not male or female, but the best way for us humans to understand this divine being is as our Father. Women, men, girls, and boys should all strive to demonstrate God's unconditional love–the divine affection of The First Source and Center, The Universal Father.

   Jesus was the Father incarnate in human form. When you see how Jesus lived, when you study what he did, you are seeing exactly what the Heavenly Father would do. *Jesus is the best way for us to understand the personality of God.* Jesus understands the Father fully because Jesus was a divine being before he came to earth to live as God and man. He is truly the Way, the Truth, and the Life.

8. **God is the creator of Jesus.** Jesus did not resist the title of "Son of God," because he came directly from The Universal Father. Although he lived as a God-man–the "Son of Man" and the "Son of God," he was a divine being before he came to earth.

   Before earth, Jesus was a divine being who carried out the Father's plan to create vast numbers of stars and planets and beings. Jesus is the Creator-Father of angels and humans in the Heavenly Father's universal family. The divine Son of God who became Jesus had already initiated a vast creative universe project and was the way, the truth, and the life to huge numbers of angels and humans across vast stretches of space over unimaginable eons of time.

He is intimately involved in his heaven and all of his creation. The Father created our Son of God to fulfill a unique role in His eternal universe plan. And Jesus taught that we have a unique part in that plan too. This is our divine birthright.

Jesus' Mission on Earth

Undoubtedly, the Divine Son who became Jesus had a very clear mission in coming to earth. And this mission was not to be a blood sacrifice to make it possible for the Father to reach us. The mission of Jesus supported his main mission to his entire universe and focused on a new revelation of God the Father. It was also for God to experience life as a human being and for Jesus to make a new revelation of man to God: God and humans need each other, need to work in partnership, to fulfill the divine plan.

Jesus was the Universal Father incarnate in human form. When we look at how Jesus lived, when we observe his actions, we are looking at exactly what God would do. **Jesus is the perfect and only way to have a full understanding of the nature and personality of God the Father.**

> . . . Have I been with you so long, and you still do not know me, Philip? Whoever has seen me has seen the Father. How can you say, "Show us the Father"?
>
> –Jesus, from *The Bible* (John 14:9)

Jesus dedicated his life to reveal how we could rely on God with total faith to meet incredible challenges. He not only gave us a perfect example, but he also painstakingly gave us his teachings so that we could learn by this example.

He wants all humankind to meet the challenge of living unique lives at every point in history within unique environments and challenges. Jesus' Spirit of Truth shows us the truth and helps us interpret his teachings so we can live true spiritual lives for our time and place.

> That which the world needs most to know is: Men are the sons of God, and through faith they can actually realize, and daily experience, this ennobling truth. My bestowal should help all men to know that they are the children of God, but such knowledge will not suffice if they fail personally to faith-grasp the saving truth that they are the living spirit sons of the eternal Father. The gospel of the kingdom is concerned with the love of the Father and the service of his children on earth.
>
> –Jesus, from *The Urantia* Book (193:0.4)

Preparing for the Earth Mission

There is no doubt that our Divine Son who became Jesus was very deliberate in picking earth. And it is clear that earth was the best place for him to give the fullest revelation of the

Universal Father and also gain the greatest comprehension of living life as a human, especially on such a troubled planet. There is also no doubt, that in a vast universe, there were other planets that our Divine Son considered.

The time, planet, the people, and the family for our Son of God were very carefully chosen. These were the greatest opportunity for him to extend his main universe mission of being the Way, the Truth, and the Life. It was the greatest opportunity for him to show the love of God and establish his eternal teachings.

Going into this earth mission, our Son of God established several key guidelines and priorities that will help us understand his life (based on *The Bible* and *The Urantia Book*):

Perfectly follow the Father's will. Our Son of God decided that as the incarnation of the Father, he would base every decision on what his Father wanted. His focus was not on himself, but on supporting his Heavenly Father. And this life example would benefit all of his children across a vast universe.

> Truly, truly, I say to you, the Son can do nothing of his own accord, but only what he sees the Father doing. For whatever the Father does, that the Son does likewise.
>
> –Jesus, from *The Bible* (John 5:19)

> Our Father in heaven, hallowed be your name. Your kingdom come, your will be done, on earth as it is in heaven . . .
>
> –Jesus, from The Bible (Matthew 6:9-10)

Set humankind free. The earth has always been filled with spiritually lost people. This is a very challenging, hard, and confusing place filled with real pain, cruelty, immense challenges, and uncertainty. Without a spiritual outlook, we become depressed and often self-destructive, mired in hopelessness. Life becomes pointless, unfair, and unfulfilling.

The Divine Son came here to help us find real spiritual freedom, to find joy and welcome all the challenges of this world. He wants us to become victorious and fulfilled with every challenge. He will save and sustain everyone who is lost and confused. His mission was and still is to set humankind free: This is the salvation he brings.

> Those who are well have no need of a physician, but those who are sick. Go and learn what this means: "I desire mercy, and not sacrifice." For I came not to call the righteous, but sinners.
>
> –Jesus, from *The Bible* (Matthew 9:12-13)

What man of you, having a hundred sheep, if he has lost one of them, does not leave the ninety-nine in the open country, and go after the one that is lost, until he finds it? And when he has found it, he lays it on his shoulders, rejoicing. And when he comes home, he calls together his friends and his neighbors, saying to them,

> "Rejoice with me, for I have found my sheep that was lost." Just so, I tell you, there will be more joy in heaven over one sinner who repents than over ninety-nine righteous persons who need no repentance.
>
> –Jesus, from *The Bible*
> (Luke 15:4-7)

Live a natural human life. The Son of God who became Jesus decided that he would live a natural human life, that he would not resort to his extraordinary power to further his plans. He would live and achieve under the same conditions and rules that all humans face. He would live as a mortal completely dedicated to the Father's will in perfect trust, as a little child trusts good parents. He would continually inspire humans for the times they live in, for all ages.

Deal with Lucifer. The rebel angel Lucifer had caused many problems by promoting false teachings. Countless numbers of angels and humans were confused and led astray. This led to terrible problems on earth that we are still trying to untangle. Lucifer knew our Son of God would have only human abilities on earth and was potentially vulnerable.

Our Divine Son knew all about this and decided to face the rebel angels that Lucifer would send: He would be a human completely reliant on the Heavenly Father. He decided to confront them as a human and take a major step in setting the affairs of earth and his universe in order. And, he triumphed.

Be a spiritual leader and teacher. Our Son of God decided to not only show us the way, but to teach us that way. He would give humankind his perfect, divine, personal religion to show us how to be reborn and come to God directly.

His goal was *not to found a church*: His goal was to give teachings that could be understood and interpreted by every person, in every time and place on earth . . . and across a vast universe.

His Spirit of Truth lives in all sincere hearts and helps all of us know and live the truth. It helps us interpret his teachings for our day and generation to meet the challenges of the present with living faith.

His mission was and is to be the Way, the Truth, and the Life.

Jesus on Earth

Our dear Son of God came into this world as all humans do, through the miracle of birth. His unique person was placed in the fetus of his mother Mary and would go through the normal human evolutionary process. He had all the challenges *and much, much more* than we face, for he was truly a man of his time and place.

As he grew, he became more and more aware of his divine nature and all his memories of his divine life before earth. He worked hard to fulfill his family and community obligations and to develop his physical, intellectual, and spiritual human gifts. He showed tremendous self-mastery in all aspects of life, especially as he began to gain access to all his divine power and vision: Before he came to earth, he made it a priority to live an entirely-natural human life, unless his Father wanted otherwise at certain times.

Jesus was the oldest child in Joseph and Mary's growing family and delighted in helping his parents and teaching his siblings. He was a remarkable Jewish man in Northern Galilee in the 1st Century under Roman occupation and the local rule of Herod Antipas. The full knowledge of His remarkable life as God and man, and his original unaltered perfect spiritual teachings, are destined to awaken and transform all willing people and to remake our entire world.

Nothing else will work: We already tried that.

He went to school and had playmates and hobbies, and developed deep friendships. He worked with his father, Joseph, and was soon a skilled craftsman and contributed as a very active member of the village of Nazareth. He enjoyed nature and the simple pleasures of life like family, friends, conversation, exercise, good food, and nature.

By the time Jesus began his pubic ministry, he was a perfected human being and was completely conscious of his divine nature and eternal memories. He was profoundly focused on finding and doing the Father's will and fulfilling his mission on earth. He was dedicated to enlightening all his earth children and those on all his other planets.

He had an incredible drive for learning and educated himself in many areas and developed good skills in several professions. He was a practical man. And he had the perfect balance of mind, body, and spirit. Jesus was the most amazing person who lived and will ever live on earth.

Jesus–The Man

Jesus' devotion to the Father's will and the service of man was even more than mortal decision and human determination; it was a wholehearted consecration of himself to such an unreserved bestowal of love . . .

You must not take the human Jesus away from men. The Master has ascended on high as a man, as well as God; he belongs to men; men belong to him. How unfortunate that religion itself should be so misinterpreted as to take the human Jesus away from struggling mortals! Let not the discussions of the humanity or the divinity of the Christ obscure the saving truth that Jesus of Nazareth was a religious man who, by faith, achieved the knowing and the doing of the will of God; he was the most truly religious man who has ever lived . . .

The time is ripe to witness the figurative resurrection of the human Jesus from his burial tomb amidst the theological traditions and the religious dogmas of nineteen centuries. Jesus of Nazareth must not be longer sacrificed to even the splendid concept of the glorified Christ . . .

To "follow Jesus" means to personally share his religious faith and to enter into the spirit of the Master's life of unselfish service for man. One of the most important things in human living is to find out what Jesus believed, to discover his ideals, and to strive for the achievement of his exalted life purpose. Of all human knowledge, that which is of greatest value is to know the religious life of Jesus and how he lived it . . .

> The common people heard Jesus gladly, and they will again respond to the presentation of his sincere human life of consecrated religious motivation if such truths shall again be proclaimed to the world. The people heard him gladly because he was one of them, an unpretentious layman; the world's greatest religious teacher was indeed a layman.
>
> –*The Urantia Book* (196.1.1)

Jesus truly knows what it is like to be a human, even though at his core, he had a divine identity with expanding, then complete memories of who he was before he came to earth, and access to his divine power. He was God and Man, but did live a truly human life.

The Human Jesus

> The Son of Man experienced those wide ranges of human emotion which reach from superb joy to profound sorrow. He

was a child of joy and a being of rare good humor; likewise was he a "man of sorrows and acquainted with grief." In a spiritual sense, he did live through the mortal life from the bottom to the top, from the beginning to the end. From a material point of view, he might appear to have escaped living through both social extremes of human existence, but intellectually he became wholly familiar with the entire and complete experience of humankind.

Jesus knows about the thoughts and feelings, the urges and impulses, of the evolutionary and ascendant mortals of the realms, from birth to death. He has lived the human life from the beginnings of physical, intellectual, and spiritual selfhood up through infancy, childhood, youth, and adulthood–even to the human experience of death . . .

And this was his true and supreme purpose. He did not come down to live on (earth) as the perfect and detailed example for any child or adult, any man or woman, in that age or any other. True it is, indeed, that in his full, rich, beautiful, and noble

> life we may all find much that is exquisitely exemplary, divinely inspiring, but this is because he lived a true and genuinely human life. Jesus did not live his life on earth in order to set an example for all other human beings to copy. He lived this life in the flesh by the same mercy ministry that you all may live your lives on earth; and as he lived his mortal life in his day and as he was, so did he thereby set the example for all of us thus to live our lives in our day and as we are. You may not aspire to live his life, but you can resolve to live your lives even as, and by the same means that, he lived his . . . Jesus is the new and living way from man to God, from the partial to the perfect, from the earthly to the heavenly, from time to eternity.
>
> – *The Urantia Book* (129.4.1)

And so, the divine Son of God who came to earth and became Jesus, lived for all peoples and nations and times on earth, and across a vast universe. No one has the right to try to control access to him or the story of his matchless life. He belongs to all of us as our Father-Brother.

We can have direct contact with him if we open our hearts to our amazing human birthright that he lived: He is the way, the truth, and the life and will bring us all to the Father of all.

The modern age will refuse to accept a religion which is inconsistent with facts and out of harmony with its highest conceptions of truth, beauty, and goodness. The hour is striking for a rediscovery of the true and original foundations of present-day distorted and compromised Christianity—the real life and teachings of Jesus.

—*The Urantia Book*
(195:9.5)

The Original Teachings of Jesus

The Lost Pre-Christian Way

Chapter 4

You're at a fork in the road: Follow the leadings of your spirit–your inner self–or rely on your current assumptions and loyalties. I challenge you to continue to keep an open mind and wholeheartedly follow the divine leading of God within: Find the new life you yearn for.

Find Jesus directly.

If you don't change your current thinking and doing, if you make the same assumptions and decisions, your life won't improve; you won't find the joyous and happy life God has for you. Walking through the gateway to that incredible life requires you to risk what you know for the new world that God wants to reveal to you.

The path to that fantastic future is the fantastic God-Man–Jesus, and the guide is his wondrous pre-Christian teachings. The life of Jesus is the ultimate revelation of the nature and love of our Father and the truths that Jesus teaches us. The only way our lives and the world will improve is when we accept the original teachings of Jesus and dedicate our lives to knowing the Father, trusting **completely** in His guidance, and serving others as Jesus serves us, as a parent.

When you express your desire for truth, the Spirit of Truth will come to you and reveal and confirm the truth. When you place loyalty to God above any religion, church, or other human institution or person, the full truth can be revealed.

In this Chapter we'll learn about the most essential teachings of Jesus in comparison to what Christianity teaches.

The Religion About Jesus and the Religion of Jesus

Before you can accept and begin to understand the true teachings of Jesus, you need to recognize that the early Christian leaders created a religion about Jesus that supplanted the true religion of Jesus. Our world is in endless, increasingly-severe turmoil because the religion of Jesus was never taught or attempted globally.

The apostle Peter began the distortion with his earliest preaching. Paul of Tarsus then formulated modern Christianity on the Jesus-focus of Peter and then his own flawed interpretations and additions of non-Jesus teachings. The result was very successful and launched a new order of human society, but has *never come close* to the benefits from the real religion of Jesus, and has led us to global crisis and the gradual devolution of civilization.

If the original teachings of Jesus were taught and lived by the early Jesus movement, the entire ancient world–globally–would have accepted them within a few centuries. Our world would be remarkably better and demonstrate so many more of the values that the Master taught.

The Christian religion about Jesus is that he is the Son of God who had to be sacrificed to make it possible for God to reach us, to compensate/atone for the sin of Adam and Eve and humankind. To remove this sin that's on our souls at birth, the Father required the blood sacrifice of Jesus. The only way to avoid hell and be saved is to believe that Jesus is Christ and saves us from original sin, the depravity of mankind, and to repent of personal sin.

The Christian focus is very often on self–the saving of ourselves, repenting of sin, self-examination to prevent sin, repenting of more sin, and finding the experience of Christ: the worshipping of Jesus. We are told we must accept Jesus, be cleansed in his blood, and follow Jesus' teachings and the guidance from a Christian church.

No wonder so many people can't fill their spiritual hunger and live in fear, and avoid seeking Jesus! **We need to liberate the name, "Jesus" from Christianity.** We need to discover his true teachings and the full spectacle of his earth life.

The *religion of Jesus* is that God is your loving Father, we are all his children, and that by faith we experience this liberating truth and are saved. By following God's leading to service, we unlock a life of joy, supreme confidence, achievement, and an eternal future of adventure and triumph that transforms personal sin into dedication to God.

Every fear and limitation of character is transformed into the secure, courageous, confident, powerful, selfless nature of a God-dedicated person.

The focus of the *religion of Jesus* is on the direct, astounding, soul-satisfying relationship with our **infinitely-loving** God, our Father, our Creator. We follow His will and give ourselves in self-forgetful service to others and are reborn and grow daily through unending levels of happiness and success.

The original teachings of Jesus are the prefect way and were *taught to him by the Universal Father–God.* But to know these truths, you must be willing to give up man-made teachings and loyalties to human authority. Trust your inner spirit to guide you now. Trust God.

> No man has taught me the truths which I declare to you. And this teaching is not mine but His who sent me. If any man really desires to do my Father's will, he shall certainly know about my teaching, whether it be God's or whether I speak for myself. He who speaks for himself seeks his own glory, but when I declare the words of the Father, I thereby seek the glory of him who sent me.
>
> –Jesus from *The Urantia Book* (166:2.1)

The Nature of God

The most liberating truths that Jesus teaches are about God. I gave you my interpretation in Chapter 3 in The Big Truths about God section. Now we'll focus on the **authoritative teaching** about God that Jesus gives. Remember: Jesus came direct from the Father and taught the truths he was taught by the Father. Understanding who God is has a profound impact on our lives.

> Out of your wrong concepts of the Father in heaven grow your false ideas of humility and springs much of your hypocrisy. Man may be a worm of the dust by nature and origin, but when he becomes indwelt by my Father's spirit, that man becomes divine in his destiny . . . the human soul of mortal man which shall have become the reborn child of this indwelling spirit shall certainly ascend with the divine spirit to the very presence of the eternal Father . . .
>
> . . . The meaningless and menial practices of an ostentatious and false humility are incompatible with the appreciation of the

> source of your salvation and the recognition of the destiny of your spirit-born souls . . .
>
> –Jesus, from *The Urantia Book* (149:6.9-10)

God is Spirit and God is Father. Jesus taught only two things about God: He is a Father when he relates to his children and that he is Spirit. Jesus never referred to the Father as a king, but as the spirit head of the spiritual brotherhood of all His children. Jesus only referred to deity by two names–God and Father. The word "father" was used when he referred to the personal relationship with God.

Jesus didn't present an organized and systematic teaching about the Father since he said that he and the Father are one: If you see Jesus, you see the Father. If you know the Son, you know the Father.

> You learn about God from Jesus by observing the divinity of his life, not by depending on his teachings. From the life of the Master you may each assimilate that

> concept of God which represents the measure of your capacity to perceive realities spiritual and divine, truths real and eternal. The finite can never hope to comprehend the Infinite except as the Infinite was focalized in . . . the human life of Jesus of Nazareth.
>
> –*The Urantia Book* (169:4.3)

Jesus is the perfect revelation of the Father's love and other divine personal traits. Jesus is the spiritual lens that makes the Father visible and understandable to human beings. Without the revelation of Jesus, we could not hope to have a good comprehension of the nature of God, of his adorable attributes, and his supreme love and caring for each of us as his little children.

It is through the life of Jesus that we truly know, that we can truly see the Father. This is the very Father who knows each of us individually and longs for a personal relationship with us to give us joy and eternal life. And it is through

Jesus that the Father teaches us his truth and gives us this life.

> You have thought that your forefathers in the wilderness ate manna–the bread of heaven–but I say to you that this was the bread of earth . . . my Father now stands ready to give you the true bread of life. The bread of heaven is that which comes down from God and gives eternal life to the men of the world . . . I am this bread of life. He who comes to me shall not hunger, while he who believes me shall never thirst . . . to those who do believe–fear not. All those led of the Father shall come to me, and he who comes to me shall in nowise be cast out.
>
> –Jesus, from *The Urantia Book* (153:2.8)

God is our personal Father. Jesus taught that God is the Father to every person and is seeking us. He wants to be our father-friend, just like Jesus wants to be our brother-friend. Our loving Father does everything in His power to help us whenever we give Him an opening–an opportunity. It doesn't matter who you are, how much wealth, fame, or power you have, the Father treats everyone the same.

God searches for those who accidentally get lost, those who are confused and blinded by the material concerns of life, and those who intentionally stray from the path. The Father is always waiting for a moment when He can get our attention and leads us back to the path of joy and soul satisfaction.

> "Think of it, my son, your brother was lost and is found; he has returned alive to us!"
>
> –Jesus, from *The Urantia Book* (169:1.13)

The most important teaching Jesus gives us is that God is our loving Father and will do all to help us realize our spiritual birthright and find eternal growth. We are cared for with a perfect, infinite affection by the very Creator of the universe, our loving heavenly Father. He does not love like a father, but *as a father.*

> You are the child, and it is your Father's kingdom you seek to enter. There is present that natural affection between every normal child and its father which insures an understanding and loving relationship, and which forever precludes all disposition to bargain for the Father's love and mercy. And the gospel you are going forth to preach has to do with a salvation growing out of the faith-realization of this very and eternal child-father relationship.
>
> –Jesus, from *The Urantia Book* (140:10.4)

God gives us His infinite love. Our Father is open and generous and does not hold back anything that we are ready for and can benefit from. The only limitation is our willingness to follow Him and our capacity to benefit from His presence and other spiritual blessings. God does not condone sin and won't tolerate rebellion, but is always looking for ways to help us wake up and grow. It all starts with the gift of faith.

> John came preaching repentance to prepare you for the kingdom; now have I come proclaiming faith, the gift of God, as the price of entrance into the kingdom of heaven. If you would but believe that my Father loves you with an infinite love, then you are in the kingdom of God.
>
> –Jesus, from *The Urantia Book* (137:8.17)

Jesus also taught that God does not willfully afflict us. We suffer from the accidents of time and the nature of this material life on earth, and our honest mistakes/errors. Then we suffer from the consequences of sin–knowingly going against the Father's will. And lastly, suffering comes from iniquity–persistent rebellion against the will of the Father. We truly reap what we sow through our decisions.

God gives us the amazing opportunity of life to embrace the full adventure of finding Him and doing His will through an eternal spiral of more joy, service, and growth.

> The Father rather desires that you draw out your heart to the hungry, and that you minister to the afflicted souls; then shall your light shine in obscurity, and even your darkness shall be as the noonday. Then shall the Lord guide you continually, satisfying your soul and renewing your strength. You shall become like a watered garden, like a spring whose waters fail not.
>
> –Jesus, from *The Urantia Book* (147:8.4)

Salvation

Finding God is the first step to an everlasting salvation. Jesus teaches the perfect way to enter the kingdom of heaven and begin real growth. We are saved with initial rebirth and maintain this salvation by working hard to follow the Father and love others as God loves us.

Entering the kingdom of heaven–the experience of the Father's presence–saves us from all fear, anxiety, selfishness, materialism, lack of motivation, and other character flaws . . . and ultimately, death itself.

All you need to do to find God and be reborn is to be hungry for the truth and sincerely come to God wholeheartedly and accept His presence with faith.

When you accept the spirit of the Father within, you become a child of God. Jesus says that all you need to do to be saved and reborn is to take time with God and use your faith to recognize His spirit that lives within you. Believe. Accept the divine experience within you, and you will know that God's spirit lives within, that you are a child of God, and that we are all brothers and sisters.

> When men and women ask what shall we do to be saved, you shall answer, Believe this gospel of the kingdom; accept divine forgiveness. By faith recognize the indwelling spirit of God, whose acceptance makes you a son of God . . .

> Salvation is the gift of the Father . . . Acceptance by faith on your part makes you a partaker of the divine nature, a son or a daughter of God. By faith you are justified; by faith are you saved; and by this same faith are you eternally advanced in

> the way of progressive and divine perfection . . . All down through the ages has this same faith saved the sons of men, but now has a Son come forth from the Father to make salvation more real and acceptable.
>
> –Jesus, from *The Urantia Book* (150:5.2-3)

When you fully accept God, you'll immediately know that He is your Father and loves you unconditionally and has forgiven all your sins. When you accept this divine forgiveness, you're filled with overflowing joy and a desire to love others in return with that same fatherly affection. You begin to be liberated.

The Kingdom of Heaven and Spiritual Liberty

The kingdom of heaven is our reward now and forever. The kingdom of heaven is the presence of God and the dedication of our lives to the doing of His will and the service to others. Jesus used the term, "kingdom of heaven" because his followers had lifelong crystallized concepts of earthly kingdoms. We can also think of this as the family of God, or other titles reflective of Jesus' teachings.

> On this afternoon the Master distinctly taught a new concept of the double nature of the kingdom in that he portrayed the following two phases:
>
> "First. The kingdom of God in this world, the supreme desire to do the will of God, the unselfish love of man which yields the good fruits of improved ethical and moral conduct.
>
> "Second. The kingdom of God in heaven, the goal of mortal believers, the estate wherein the love for God is perfected, and wherein the will of God is done more divinely."
>
> –*The Urantia Book* (170:2.17-20)

Jesus taught that the kingdom of heaven must focus on the fatherhood of God and the brotherhood of man and leads to amazing spiritual liberty. This focus liberates us from fear and brings new endowments:

---

1. The possession of new courage and augmented spiritual power. The gospel of the kingdom was to set man free and inspire him to dare to hope for eternal life.
2. The gospel carried a message of new confidence and true consolation for all men, even for the poor.
3. It was in itself a new standard of moral values, a new ethical yardstick wherewith to measure human conduct. It portrayed the ideal of a resultant new order of human society.
4. It taught the pre-eminence of the spiritual compared with the material; it glorified spiritual realities and exalted superhuman ideals.
5. This new gospel held up spiritual attainment as the true goal of living. Human life received a new endowment of moral value and divine dignity.
6. Jesus taught that eternal realities were the result (reward) of righteous earthly striving. Man's mortal sojourn

> on earth acquired new meanings consequent upon the recognition of a noble destiny.
>
> 7. The new gospel affirmed that human salvation is the revelation of a far-reaching divine purpose to be fulfilled and realized in the future destiny of the endless service of the salvaged sons of God.
>
> – *The Urantia Book* (170:2-5)

Forgiveness, Spiritual Growth, and Service

Jesus taught that God forgives us even before we think to ask. He doesn't require anything to love and forgive us, but we cannot experience His full love *until* we forgive others. Once you are reborn and feel the presence and initial love of God, you must move forward to understand and forgive others. *This is the only way to experience the full depth of God's love for you.*

There are four essential steps of inner righteousness to experience God's forgiveness, according to Jesus:

---

1. God's forgiveness is made actually available and is personally experienced by man just in so far as he forgives his fellows.
2. Man will not truly forgive his fellows unless he loves them as himself.
3. To thus love your neighbor as yourself is the highest ethics.
4. Moral conduct, true righteousness, becomes, then, the natural result of such love.

. . . The true and inner religion of the kingdom unfailingly and increasingly tends to manifest itself in practical avenues of social service. Jesus taught a living religion that impelled its believers to engage in the doing of loving service.

–*The Urantia Book*
(170:3.4-8)

If you want to find all the joys of the religion of Jesus, you need to help others to do the same and solve real problems. Once you are reborn, once you are saved, God expects you to give his love to others in *self-forgetful* service. We are expected to grow as spiritual adults. This manifestation of the love of the Father is the essence of the religion of Jesus and the secret to spiritual progress here on earth and in the afterlife.

This eternal cycle begins with accepting the love of God, following His guidance, and forgiving others to release the love of God through self-forgetful service. Since we know that God accepts and loves us *unconditionally*, we are released from fear and the need to selfishly over-analyze and examine ourselves, obsessing with salvation.

Our only concern is to find and do the will of the Father. We trust and follow him with the complete devotion of little children. We assume we are saved and focus on others.

> Seek first the kingdom of God, and when you have found entrance thereto, all things needful shall be added to you. Be not, therefore, unduly anxious for the morrow.
>
> –Jesus, from *The Urantia Book* (140:6.13)

> My kingdom is founded on love, proclaimed in mercy, and established by unselfish service.
>
> –Jesus, from *The Urantia Book* (155:1.2)

The purpose of life is clear, simple, and transcendent. Once we accept the reality of God within, once we accept that we are children of God, we can begin to realize our destinies. Again, our only purpose is to find and do the Father's will.

> And Nicodemus said: "But how can I begin to lay hold upon this spirit which is to remake me in preparation for entering into the kingdom?" Jesus answered:

"Already does the spirit of the Father in heaven indwell you. If you would be led by this spirit from above, very soon would you begin to see with the eyes of the spirit, and then by the wholehearted choice of spirit guidance would you be born of the spirit since your only purpose in living would be to do the will of your Father who is in heaven. And so finding yourself born of the spirit and happily in the kingdom of God, you would begin to bear in your daily life the abundant fruits of the spirit."

–*The Urantia Book* (142:6.7)

The only way to fully follow the leading of God is to understand and forgive others so we can release the Father's love through our selfless service. We can't just try really hard to love someone without the step of listening and understanding them. Jesus taught that the manifestation of love shows maturity and means that we have forgiven others.

When a wise man understands the inner impulses of his fellows, he will love them.

> And when you love your brother, you have already forgiven him. This capacity to understand man's nature and forgive his apparent wrongdoing is Godlike . . .
>
> Your inability or unwillingness to forgive your fellows is the measure of your immaturity, your failure to attain adult sympathy, understanding, and love. You hold grudges and nurse vengefulness in direct proportion to your ignorance of the inner nature and true longings of your children and your fellow beings. Love is the outworking of the divine and inner urge of life. It is founded on understanding, nurtured by unselfish service, and perfected in wisdom.
>
> –Jesus, from *The Urantia Book* (174:1.4-5)

The real teachings of Jesus show that with the foundation of direct contact with the Father, we are awakened and set free to find and do His will. We're empowered to the fullest extent to go into the outer world of error, evil, and sin to transform it. God gives us the incredible adventure of uncertainty of the outcome, but the *total certainty* that following His guidance is the key to all.

> There is no adventure in the course of mortal existence more enthralling than to enjoy the exhilaration of becoming the material life partner with spiritual energy and divine truth in one of their triumphant struggles with error and evil. It is a marvelous and transforming experience to become the living channel of spiritual light to the mortal who sits in spiritual darkness.
>
> –Jesus, from *The Urantia Book* (130:2.4)

When you discover and follow the original pre-Christian teachings of Jesus, you are truly set free as a liberated son or daughter of the Universal Father. You are reborn as you are enveloped in the infinitely-loving embrace of God and the thrilling adventure of this life partnership. You are ready to make the decisions that will echo through your eternal future.

Evil, Sin, and Iniquity

As we reviewed in the last chapter, Jesus never taught that sin was a substance or a debt that was inherited or accumulated; sin is not a tangible or even mystical material that encases or blocks the soul. This kind of primitive superstition comes from humankind's earliest days and led to endless efforts to appease God with many types of sacrifices including food, clothing, animals, and worst of all, innocent men, women, and children.

The belief in sin as a mystical substance that must be removed at any cost is based on repugnant and very backward ideas about God. The Creator is thought of as an angry God (almost a force of nature) that must be appeased through the suffering and destruction of things and people. And primitive humans based their ideas about God on how nature behaved. Combined with their dreamlife and imaginations, primitive religion and the idea of karma and sin were born.

In this worldview, God's way of molding humans is through punishment and the paying of debts to Him, and He doesn't care who pays the debt. God looks more like a warlord or crime boss. And, unfortunately, the Christian view of Jesus rests on this barbaric, backward, and revolting view of our loving heavenly Father.

Jesus actually taught that God loves each of us individually and wants all of us to accept His divine presence and begin to live His will to realize joy and an amazing destiny. When we accept our Father, we are led to love Him, and we make the only purpose of our lives to do His will.

Of course, no matter how well-intentioned, we make mistakes, we make errors, we make *evil* choices. When we know what the Father wants us to do and still choose our own way, then our choice is *sinful*. Jesus defined errors as *evil* and conscious defiance as *sin*. He also taught that if we work with all our hearts against the will of God, that these choices are *iniquitous* and lead to soul death.

Jesus taught these laws of relating ourselves to the Father's will:

> Evil is the unconscious or unintended transgression of the divine law, the Father's will. Evil is likewise the measure of the imperfectness of obedience to the Father's will.
>
> Sin is the conscious, knowing, and deliberate transgression of the divine law, the Father's will. Sin is the measure of unwillingness to be divinely led and spiritually directed.
>
> Iniquity is the willful, determined, and persistent transgression of the divine law, the Father's will. Iniquity is the measure of the continued rejection of the Father's loving plan of personality survival and the Sons' merciful ministry of salvation.
>
> –Jesus, from *The Urantia Book* (148:4.3-5)

Ultimately, it is our choice in relation to the Father's will that determines if we progress forward with God or go backward into darkness and death. There is no hell, but we can actually destroy our souls and never find eternal life after we die on earth. When we choose to do the Father's will, we grow and lay claim to the amazing birthright of eternal life and realize significant personal benefits here and now.

Prayer and Worship

Jesus taught that prayer is the most effective thing we can do to find and be able to follow God's will. Prayer is the primary way that we open ourselves up to change and are able to receive the power and insights from God. Prayer increases our capacity for God and stimulates us to action to improve our lives and those of others. Once we are reborn, prayer is the gateway to spiritual nourishment and guidance.

The purpose of prayer is to change us, not to change God. Prayer should lead to thanksgiving which should lead to worship of God, the divine embrace. Jesus taught that worship is when we express our love and appreciation for the Father without expecting or asking for anything in return. We forget ourselves in the astounding presence of God.

Prayer is self-reminding–sublime thinking; worship is self-forgetting–superthinking. Worship is effortless attention, true and ideal soul rest, a form of restful spiritual exertion.

–*The Urantia Book* (143:7.7)

Prayer is entirely a personal and spontaneous expression of the attitude of the soul toward the spirit; prayer should be the communion of sonship and the expression of fellowship. Prayer, when indited by the spirit, leads to co-operative spiritual progress. The ideal prayer is a form of spiritual communion which leads to intelligent worship. True praying is the sincere attitude of reaching heavenward for the attainment of your ideals.

Prayer is the breath of the soul and should lead you to be persistent in your attempt to ascertain the Father's will . . .

–Jesus, from *The Urantia Book* (144:2.2-3)

When we think of the wonderful spiritual challenge of the religion of Jesus, the invitation to know and do the Father's will, the liberation of truth, the joy of serving others, we realize that *true prayer is the only technique that is valid.* No substitute will work. No distraction will change the reality of this wonderful spiritual alchemy. If we want to realize our individual spiritual birthrights, if we want to live the true religion of Jesus, we must pray.

The Life You Were Meant to Live

To accept and live the true religion of Jesus is to use your sincere hunger for truth and gift of faith to believe that you are a child of our Universal Father, and then to dedicate your life to following Him wherever He takes you, whatever he wants you to do. As Jesus said, if you do this, *everything needed for your spiritual welfare will be provided.* And you will find the incredible, almost unimaginable life that you were meant to live.

If you believe the essential truth that you are a child of God, you will be set free to begin the journey. If you continue to spend time with

God and seek the truth, He will increasingly reveal all that you can comprehend to expand your spiritual liberation as a daughter or son of God. You will be able to transcend all limitations of character and begin to grow a true spiritual, eternal character–your soul.

Your fears will begin to fade as you begin to serve others with a superhuman affection–the love of your Divine Parent. You will have deep soul satisfaction and a life of real accomplishments and joys. You will see more and more of who you will be in eternity. If you are willing to follow the true teachings of Jesus, everything about you will change more than you ever thought possible.

> The religion of Jesus does, indeed, dominate and transform its believers, demanding that men dedicate their lives to seeking for a knowledge of the will of the Father in heaven and requiring that the energies of living be consecrated to the

> unselfish service of the brotherhood of man.
>
> –*The Urantia Book* (195:9.6)

And so, Jesus gave us the greatest commandment and privilege of all:

> You well know the commandment which directs that you love one another; that you love your neighbor even as yourself. But I am not wholly satisfied with even that sincere devotion on the part of my children. I would have you perform still greater acts of love in the kingdom of the believing brotherhood. And so I give you this new commandment: That you love one another even as I have loved you. And by this will all men know that you are my disciples if you thus love one another.
>
> When I give you this new commandment, I do not place any new burden upon your souls; rather do I bring you new joy and make it possible for you to experience new pleasure in knowing the delights of the bestowal of your heart's affection upon

> your fellow men. I am about to experience the supreme joy, even though enduring outward sorrow, in the bestowal of my affection upon you and your fellow mortals.
>
> When I invite you to love one another, even as I have loved you, I hold up before you the supreme measure of true affection, for greater love can no man have than this: that he will lay down his life for his friends. And you are my friends; you will continue to be my friends if you are but willing to do what I have taught you. You have called me Master, but I do not call you servants. If you will only love one another as I am loving you, you shall be my friends, and I will ever speak to you of that which the Father reveals to me.
>
> –Jesus, from *The Urantia Book* (180:1.1-3)

Jesus is the total revelation of the truth through his teachings and the way he lived the truth and revealed God.

He is the Way, the Truth, and the Life.

To "follow Jesus" means to personally share his religious faith and to enter into the spirit of the Master's life of unselfish service for man. One of the most important things in human living is to find out what Jesus believed, to discover his ideals, and to strive for the achievement of his exalted life purpose. Of all human knowledge, that which is of greatest value is to know the religious life of Jesus and how he lived it.

—*The Urantia Book*
(196:1.3)

Living With Jesus Without Christianity

Total Liberation, Joy, and Triumph

Chapter 5

You probably picked up this book because you were curious about a Jesus without the Christian institution and its many denominations and churches. We've taken a new path and learned about how Christianity misinterpreted, distorted, and added to the original teachings of Jesus and warped and contaminated our understanding of him and his mission.

While the Christian religion did bring the most advanced teachings about God ever known, it also brought a misunderstanding of the nature of God and a distortion of how we relate to and live with him. The impact has been profound and led to many negative consequences and a tremendous loss of progress for humankind . . . and each individual.

Most people have no idea who Jesus really was, how he lived, what he really taught, who he is now, and his relation to Christianity.

The Impact

Christianity at its best has tiny fragments of the majesty and perfection of the original teachings of Jesus. And yet, even as a faint echo and distortion, it led to the amazing flowering of modern Western civilization. It ushered in an unprecedented advancement in human morals and societal ethics and the creation of institutions for the common good. And there was also significant improvement for the treatment and status of women and children.

The life and teachings of Jesus are the hidden and unappreciated source and inspiration for these advancements. **It is only through a clear and complete view of and dedication to the real Jesus and his teachings that we can improve ourselves and the world.** We've tried everything else and are descending into chaos, cultural disintegration, devolution, and global disaster.

I'm convinced that the apostles of Jesus and early leaders were absolutely sincere and did not fully understand the impact of the changes and compromises they made. Thousands of them gave their lives in unspeakable deaths just to spread the truth that Jesus was resurrected and is our Son of God. But, while you might honor their dedication and sacrifice, *our loyalty must ultimately be to God* above any human being or group or church.

I am sure that those heroes would agree.

This is our time and place. This is our responsibility.

Going to Jesus Directly

Everyone–including Christians–deserve to know the truth that Jesus brought from the Father. It is time to embrace Jesus directly and study his original teachings and life. We need to come back to that real truth to find the future that our Son of God wants for us. We need to take responsibility to search for truth, not blindly and passively accept what we are told.

We need to go to the SOURCE.

Our Son of God will not tolerate anyone who seeks to be a middleman or wants to distort his original teachings. Our divine Master wants to know you directly, and so does the Father–the Creator.

Our divine Son of God created and governs a vast universe under the guidance of the Universal Father. He has unimaginable power and is a perfect manifestation of the Father's love and adorable character. And, in all that vast creation, he chose earth to live the astounding spectacle of God incarnate.

As Jesus, as the Son of Man, he revealed the nature of God. Jesus is the best way we can understand the person of the Father. Our Son of God is the Way, the Truth, and the Life.

Jesus taught that God is our loving Father and knows each of us. He will give us all we need through His spirit inside of each of us. If we *hunger for growth and truth*, to find God and salvation, we need to wholeheartedly and sincerely accept the spirit within. We need to use our *faith* to believe we are the children of God and then to forgive and serve others.

We need to dedicate our lives to the eternal adventure of a relationship with God and discovering and following His will. We are to manifest, to create better lives and a better world. We are to love others as Jesus loved us, as a parent loves a child.

We need to come home to God's spirit within and begin the journey to the very source of that spirit–our Universal Father. And the bridge, the gateway to that journey is our Son of God who was called "Jesus."

> It should not be the aim of kingdom believers literally to imitate the outward life of Jesus in the flesh but rather to share his faith; to trust God as he trusted God and to believe in men as he believed in men. Jesus never argued about either the fatherhood of God or the brotherhood of men; he was a living illustration of the one and a profound demonstration of the other.
>
> –*The Urantia Book* (196:1.5)

Be unafraid to claim your birthright to discover God directly. Grow that relationship. Make your own decisions and chart your own faith adventure with God as your captain. Embrace the Master and his teachings directly. Risk everything and you will gain everything.

Motivation from Jesus

I hope that I've given you some helpful instruction and a lot of inspiration. But I know someone who can do a much better job. Here is a collection of inspirational quotations from Jesus from the vast collection in *The Urantia Book*. Let them sink into your heart. Let your soul be refreshed. Let your mind respond to the Spirit of Truth of our Son of God.

Jesus teaches us that the Father knows and loves each of us:

> But I have come among you to proclaim a greater truth, one which many of the later prophets also grasped, that God loves you–every one of you–as individuals. All these generations have you had a national or racial religion; now have I come to give you a personal religion.
>
> –*The Urantia Book* (145:2.4)

Jesus teaches about the real way to salvation:

> Believe this gospel of the kingdom; accept divine forgiveness. By faith recognize the

> indwelling spirit of God, whose acceptance makes you a son of God.
>
> –*The Urantia Book* (150:5.2)

Jesus teaches about the assurance that the spirit of the Father within can give us if we accept:

> Every earth child who follows the leading of this spirit shall eventually know the will of God, and he who surrenders to the will of my Father shall abide forever. The way from the earth life to the eternal estate has not been made plain to you, but there is a way, there always has been, and I have come to make that way new and living. He who enters the kingdom has eternal life already–he shall never perish.
>
> –*The Urantia Book* (146:3.7)

When on the way to Rome, Jesus had a long talk with a sad young man about people who had become spiritually lost. He referred to the Jewish story of Jonah and the whale:

> No matter into what great depths they may have fallen, when they seek the light with a whole heart, the spirit of the Lord God of heaven will deliver them from their captivity; the evil circumstances of life will spew them out upon the dry land of fresh opportunities for renewed service and wiser living.
>
> – *The Urantia Book* (130:1.2)

When Jesus was hiking in the mountains of Crete, he helped a very depressed young man:

> I well know you wish to be left alone with your disconsolation; but it would be neither kind nor fair for me to receive such generous help from you as to how best to find my way to Phenix and then unthinkingly to go away from you . . .
>
> Sit down with me while I tell you of the service trails and happiness highways which lead from the sorrows of self to the joys of loving activities in the brotherhood of men and in the service of the God of heaven . . .

> This day, my son, you are to be reborn, re-established as a man of faith, courage, and devoted service to man, for God's sake. And when you become so readjusted to life within yourself, you become likewise readjusted to the universe; you have been born again–born of the spirit–and henceforth will your whole life become one of victorious accomplishment. Trouble will invigorate you; disappointment will spur you on; difficulties will challenge you; and obstacles will stimulate you. Arise, young man! Say farewell to the life of cringing fear and fleeing cowardice. Hasten back to duty and live your life in the flesh as a son of God, a mortal dedicated to the ennobling service of man on earth and destined to the superb and eternal service of God in eternity.
>
> –*The Urantia Book* (130:6.2)

Jesus talked to a man who worked for an unfair boss. When this shipyard worker shared his troubles, Jesus had very good advice:

> Since you know the ways of kindness and value justice, perhaps the Gods have brought this erring man near that you may lead him into this better way. Maybe you are the salt which is to make this brother more agreeable to all other men; that is, if you have not lost your savor . . . It is a marvelous and transforming experience to become the living channel of spiritual light to the mortal who sits in spiritual darkness.
>
> –*The Urantia Book* (130:2.4)

Jesus once explained to another person why he spent so much time helping others:

> Ganid, no man is a stranger to one who knows God. In the experience of finding the Father in heaven you discover that all men are your brothers, and does it seem strange that one should enjoy the exhilaration of meeting a newly discovered brother? To become acquainted with one's brothers and sisters, to know their

> problems and to learn to love them, is the supreme experience of living.
>
> –*The Urantia Book* (130:2.6)

When Jesus was in Rome, he spoke to a Roman soldier when they walked along the Tiber river:

> Be brave of heart as well as of hand. Dare to do justice and be big enough to show mercy. Compel your lower nature to obey your higher nature as you obey your superiors. Revere goodness and exalt truth. Choose the beautiful in place of the ugly. Love your fellows and reach out for God with a whole heart, for God is your Father in heaven.
>
> –*The Urantia Book* (132:4.6)

And, in one of Jesus' appearances after his resurrection, he said:

> Peace be upon you. You rejoice to know that I am the resurrection and the life, but this will avail you nothing unless you are first born of the eternal spirit, thereby coming to possess, by faith, the gift of eternal life. If you are the faith sons of my Father, you shall never die; you shall not perish. The gospel of the kingdom has taught you that all men are the sons of God. And this good news concerning the love of the heavenly Father for his children on earth must be carried to all the world. The time has come when you worship God neither on Gerizim nor at Jerusalem, but where you are, as you are, in spirit and in truth. It is your faith that saves your souls. Salvation is the gift of God to all who believe they are his sons. But be not deceived; while salvation is the free gift of God and is bestowed upon all who accept it by faith, there follows the experience of bearing the fruits of this spirit life as it is lived in the flesh. The acceptance of the doctrine of the fatherhood of God implies that you also freely accept the associated

> truth of the brotherhood of man. And if man is your brother, he is even more than your neighbor, whom the Father requires you to love as yourself. Your brother, being of your own family, you will not only love with a family affection, but you will also serve as you would serve yourself. And you will thus love and serve your brother because you, being my brethren, have been thus loved and served by me.
>
> –*The Urantia* Book (193:1.2)

Your Future with Jesus

All of us can have a direct connection and relationship with Jesus and the Father without any middleman. You can contact him anytime, anywhere, in any situation. It should also be obvious that the best source of the teachings of Jesus is the Master himself: He gave his Spirit of Truth to continue teaching us.

Many people might tell you that you need to let them interpret Jesus for you. Many people might say that you have a duty to Christianity or another group. Many people might want you to agree with them, even though your soul is leading you to explore the truth and make your own conclusions.

But remember: **God accepts you and loves you unconditionally.** All you need to do to start is to accept his presence, spend time with Him, and follow his leading. Once you fully accept God, you have the peace, assurance, and security to seek the truth and follow Him. Once you follow the leading of the Spirit of Truth from our Son of God, you will be brought to the Father's spirit within you and the gateway to eternity.

Nothing else will satisfy the hunger that God placed in your soul. You can't have someone do this for you. You have to actively and bravely take the adventure of truth-discovery and living.

No matter how much a church or group has given you, no matter how much you trust and admire someone, **God expects you to depend on Him and follow Him**. God expects you to take responsibility for your life and risk all for Him.

And once you step through that door with faith, you will be infused with total joy and liberated for confident action and success. Once you spend time with our Son of God each day, you will learn more and more truth and be able to adapt to any challenge. Once you work with our Son of God and the Father, you will begin to live your destiny.

You will come home to your Divine Father and give all that you are to Him. And He will lead you to endless exploration, challenge, transformation, and success. You will triumph over every obstacle. You will overcome every weakness. You will become more like God.

You will become part of the growing planetary transformation of the faith-children of God, the children of our Son of God. Jesus is here and teaching us now. The Spirit of Truth is gradually organizing, directing, teaching, and activating all who want to know God. In every place on earth, in every culture, race, religion, and nation, God is activating anyone who is willing to help.

An astounding age of spiritual progress is coming. The hunger for knowledge about Jesus is intensifying. Untold millions are yearning for the truth and a direct relationship with the Master–our Son of God.

Jesus needs all of us to transform our lives and transform this world. He gave us the teachings and spiritual source to do it. He believes in you and me, and if we follow, we'll never be defeated. We'll help humankind heal the old world and build the new one.

So, let's all join together on this incredible adventure–a destiny that was planned for us before this world was made. Believe you are a child of God. Accept His presence, forgiveness, and total unconditional love. Study and embrace the original teachings of Jesus, but, most of all, embrace our Son of God and learn from him each day.

You are a son or daughter of God, and we are all family. Allow yourself to be liberated. Keep your mind open. Risk comfort. Risk social acceptance. TRUST God fully, and you will be free.

Let our Son of God lead you to an astounding adventure in this life and to the gateway of an eternal destiny as a faith child of God, the Universal Father, the Creator, your loving Dad. Together, we will join our Divine Leader, our Son of God, in joyous and successful service for the family of God: the kingdom of heaven.

Let's transform ourselves each day.

Let's transform the world.

Come home and be reborn. Come home to the life you were meant to live.

Find and follow the Master.

LIVE.

Join My List, Ask a Question

Visit: FindMyNewLife.com

If you enjoyed this book, you'll be glad to know I've got another book that'll be released soon, and other projects after that. As soon as I have something I think you'd like, I'll send you an alert. Of course, you can get off the list at any time.

So, **please sign up today**. I'm looking forward to sharing more with you to help you on your journey. If you want to ask a question or make suggestions for a new offering, just let me know.

FindMyNewLife.com

Author's Message

It's really been a thrill to share this book with you, and I hope it's helped you on your spiritual journey. We're really all family of the same Creator, and I wish you the very best spiritual growth and personal success.

I know that whatever challenges you face, you can find peace and inspiration from God within. Things can get better. You can begin to live the life God meant for you.

You're unique and have a unique set of God-given gifts. You can find a better, more elevated life. It will bring you a new happiness and peace beyond your dreams: This is the life of real spiritual discovery with the real God.

I'll see you on the web and in my other projects.

All the best,

–Chris

About the Author

Who I Am

I'm a spiritual seeker–just like you–and do my best to follow my inner guidance. I have my struggles and challenges, but, I have complete faith that if I follow my inner light, things will be fine. God will take care of all my spiritual needs and give me the strength to face all my life challenges.

My mission is to write and speak to help people liberate themselves from everything that blocks or slows their spiritual awakening and progress.

Where I Live, What I've Done

I live in the Western United States and enjoy getting out to hike, backpack, bike ride, ski, and rock climb. Of course, friends and family are my biggest joy. This is my foundation.

I began my spiritual search in 1979 and have been involved in writing, speaking, and teaching since then. I published my first small book in 1992– *The Little Spiritual Answer*

Book, and another small book in 1993–*God Without the Garbage* (both out of print).

I've worked as an elementary school teacher, high-tech salesman, a training designer, and–of course–a writer. I'm very excited about many new book projects to come.

Other Author Books

Profound Prayer:
A Modern Prayer Guide for Peace, Power, and Personal Transformation

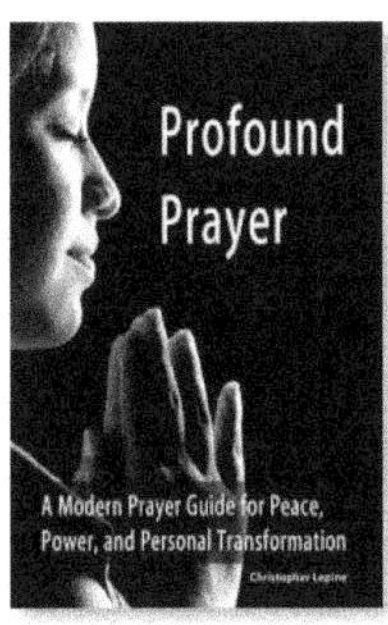

The Universal Spiritual Way:
A Complete Roadmap to a New Personal Life and a New Era for Humankind

www.ingramcontent.com/pod-product-compliance
Lightning Source LLC
LaVergne TN
LVHW010949110826
845149LV00015B/3272

* 9 7 8 1 9 6 4 8 2 2 0 0 6 *